W9-ADX-978

Friends and Assassins

Other Books by Heather Ross Miller

Fiction

The Edge of the Woods
Tenants of the House
Gone a Hundred Miles
A Spiritual Divorce and Other Stories
Confessions of a Champeen Fire Baton Twirler
La Jupe Espagnol

Poetry

The Wind Southerly
Horse Horse, Tyger Tyger
Adam's First Wife
Hard Evidence

Friends and Assassins ❧

Poems by
Heather Ross Miller

University of Missouri Press
Columbia and London

University of Missouri Press, Columbia, Missouri 65201
Printed and bound in the United States of America
5 4 3 2 1   97 96 95 94 93

Library of Congress Cataloging-in-Publication Data

Miller, Heather Ross, 1939–
    Friends and assassins : poems / by Heather Ross Miller.
    p. cm.
    ISBN 0–8262–0828–2 (cloth : alk. paper). — ISBN 0–8262–0829–0
(paper : alk. paper)
    I. Title.
PS3563.I38F73 1992
811'.54—dc20   92–35984
                                                                          CIP

⊗™ This paper meets the requirements of theAmerican
National Standard for Permanence of Paper for Printed
Library Materials, Z39.48, 1984.

Designer: Rhonda Miller
Printer and Binder: Thomson-Shore, Inc.
Typeface: Goudy

Some of these poems have appeared, some in slightly
different form, in the following magazines: *The Chariton Review,*
Kentucky Poetry Review, *The Laurel Review,* *The New Virginia Review,*
Shenandoah, *The Southern Review.*

The author is grateful to the University of Arkansas for the generous
off-campus grant in 1991 that allowed her to complete this book.

For Bill, Jim, John, Michael, Miller, Skip,
and for the memory of John Clellon Holmes

Contents ❧

I

Objects in mirror are closer than they appear ❧

Seventh Grades

We spread in the grass and slit clover
with a thumbnail, slid one stem
through another, hinged like long lovers,
locked death mates, sucking
the tight white knots
of dead persistent flowers.
We said we'd have it all,
bridesmaids, babies,
hot abundant nectars
the magazines promised like Aretha
singing off our mother's radios,
chainchain-chain!
            chainchain-
chain! Chain of fooooools!

That was our flowering period,
unlucky three-leafed,
each one an unwed
troublesome weed
of a girl
growing April through October,
chaining clover, easy as cattle
in good pasture.

Tap Water

My father wants the water tested.
He thinks it makes my mother crazy,
minerals and poisons, something seeping
off the land, something creeping up on her
when she sips that morning cup, something
making her stare. "Are you that man
who took me to the beach? Did we have
any children?"

Like things flammable and fatal
to swallow, like fortune-telling,
tap water scares the hell out of him,
but he's got to know, got to drink and find out
where she goes at night, what perpetual demons
follow.

The people in white suits collect vials,
one from the yard, another from the kitchen,
they fill out forms my father signs
and they drive off. He blinks
at the puddles in the sink.
My mother polishes her small hands,
one over the other, one over the other,
some compulsive braiding,
some intense and clinging puzzle,
one over the other,
one over the other, one—

I want to interrupt that desperate water,
drop things in and shake the vials, watch the clear
cloud back the green, the virulent blue,
distill my father back my mother,
a familiar strong
uninjured girl.

Loss of Memory

Things were going to come out of her mind someday.
Big loud things. And soft ones. Ones smelling
like honeysuckle bright in the shade, sweet,
strangling.

Things were going to take hold,
The soft blond hair of her children,
her face in their hair, her mind swelling,
the taste of salt. She would remember
her children. She would remember
the honeysuckle. She would remember
the big loud things, letters of some alphabet
and bright obnoxious multiplication tables, *and!*
the voices of her own mind shouting back at her
A B C D! Then the blond,
the soft strangle,
the unsayable sweet tangle
of her mind.

In Danger

Next to my mother's zinnia bed,
a fat old man, bald as a snail,
B.V.D.'d and barefoot,
stuffs a wicker chair.
Its dull brown flange flares around him
so that he looks like a dead petunia
or a baby giant,
and his Fatima cigar glows bright as zinnias,
the little red eyes of a tropical bird.
I am in danger.
He puts the cigar to my arm
and it burns like a little biting snake.
He hates me, whispers, "Whatcha say?"

I am nine years old, back home in Badin,
with a good tan and all expressions of shame.
The little biting snake
burns me to death, hurts like a kick
or a joke. I am in danger.
He knows my name.

Sister Narcissus, Twin Death
for Dabney Stuart

His large creeping stems
buried at the bottom of cola water
anchored a lake full, a moon full
of soft floating faces, her common lotus,
tempting faces, petals opening
toward a wild yellow ripening,
rich as butter her mother churned,
rich as braid on her brother's
Seabees jacket, slow-moving,
letting loose seeds
underwater.

This was something she needed
to keep check on, feral and strong, something
with hands to pull her down under
where she liked, deep in cola water
to her brother, to the stems,
to the long cool grab of him.

She put her lips to the lotus,
her soft yellow scent a rapture
kissing back, leaving
a strange unidentified grit,
a wild claw in the gut, a spectacular
hairline fracture through her bones,
sinews, and deep deep blood,
until
she sank in his thick cola mud
and drank up her brother
other other other.

Marooned

She wanted
one good-looking man
to get her off this place,
tear down the screen door
to give her earrings, cold wine, and shoes.
This man she wanted in a Seabees jacket
commanded campfires, harbors, airfields.
He built naval aviation things
and defended them, driving battalions
down the bright wild coast.
She nested in his arms,
a gold pet, all night,
then got up thinking, *I am one hell
of a woman, I am.*

Seabees tearing down the screen door!
coming ashore bright and loud as trumpets!
messing up the long smooth sand!
She languished for it, languished,
then got up and cursed. The gold pet
bronzed off and lurked, ugly little
succubus, an abortion in a bottle.
The desolate harbors and airfields,
her old bombed-out facilities, laughed
as she tracked the cannibal campfires,
no way to get off the island.

Dorothy Alice Receives the Word

Thinking her single years were okay,
thinking it was good to be a tough tall woman,
she opened the medicine cabinet
and saw a Drink Me bottle.
Its rich swallow mellowed the soapy day,
its dark kick dissolved away to sweet nothings,
then it talked: *Sweetheart,*
it had a voice like a therapist,
Sweetheart, I insist you are too old
to run down rabbit holes. You are too big
to play. You want a normal run-of-the-mill guy,
you want to get married, have three kids, a house
with birdbaths, barbecues, and Buicks.
Honeybunch, it was beginning to talk tough,
Honeybunch, a woman must not trust her Oz stuff
too much. A little snort of wonderland is enough.

Shut up, she said, *I like it here, I mean to stay,*
and stepping back, fell into her tub full of poppies.
The chlorinated water steaming like Kansas
offered up little bald-headed wizards, little gods
dreaming her perfectly begotten classic
and undefiled name—*there's no place*—
until she floated, one ear to the drain, *home again*
home again home home home.

Full Color

In your own room, your first room,
the pithy beaverboards skinned in creamy paint
named *Fire Glow*, *Silhouette*, *Shadow*,
and *Adoration*, their nailheads like navels
kept something out, you didn't know what,
except your mother, especially.
Your pale room at 86 Spruce, the glass kidney
under the mild mirror and the little pink fuzz of rug
thrown to the floor by the bed, cuddled you,
but the bed your mother saw in *Better Homes & Gardens*,
her own magazine bed, perfect and bewildered,
was a danger bed, devouring bed,
bed prayed in, then escaped.

In your next rooms, your weddings
and babies, the rooms with men,
perfect and bewildered and withstood,
more dangerous and devouring,
you kept something in for good.
Finally your own room again, old,
personal as a fingerprint, whorls
and hangnails intact.

Now you fashion your last room,
the chambered beating thing,
muscular as a boy, into some desperate
loving invincible lie, *Crushed Spice*,
Sweet Butter, *Blush*, *and Gossamer*—
half-believing, you lean out
to dry your hair in a coloring sun
that hurries the magazine prince,
the darling swindler,
up your fragrant stair.

What You See in the Mirror
for Fred Chappell

Objects in mirror are closer
than they appear. This is a warning
we must remember next time
when, after periods of declining health,
we recover to stand and peer at our
silvered selves.
Objects are closer. At that time,
three fates like three black sisters
named Regina, Omega, and Elise—
you don't have to remember this,
their names don't count—
nevertheless,
they swirl silk, the scent of narcissus,
cut black swathes a mile wide,
and we drown and drown and drown.
Our own remarkable fault.
That's death.

The little girl climbed through,
shocked at the first cool grasp
around her bone, then thrilled, loved,
taken up by it, plunged head and shoulders,
as they say, whole hog,
and stayed. That was Alice of the looking-glass,
Alice of the adventures, Alice of the wonderful
wonderful land, a dream, she said at the end,
a long fall down the hole.

In the Natural Course of Things

The day a pony he tried to ride
slung my brother under the Buick,
he bled red across the black asphalt
and I ran upstairs to tell my mother
who said she had a sick headache
and go call the goddamn Rescue Squad.

They sirened over and took a look
at my brother and his blood, said,
How come you let a pony sling you
under a Buick? He said, I don't know,
shut up. And dabbed a finger
in his own blood, staring at it
like it might explain.

In Head Start,
my brother couldn't leave little girls'
long blond hair alone, kept reaching
reaching reaching after something
in their long blond hair not he,
not anybody,
not even they,
could name. He plunged his fingers in,
the little girls shrilled, he pulled
his fingers back
to stare, then willed himself
in their hair all blond again
again again.

After the Rescue Squad
took my brother to an emergency room,
I stood looking at his blood
still bleeding red across the black asphalt.
Shut up, it said. Stick in your finger,
give it a blond name, pull again
again again.

November 11 in England, Remembrance Day

With fifty days, *fifty!*
left in the year, children and old ladies
brought red wreaths to the gray commons,
left them to shock me.
Pimento-paper tongues and tendrils
battered the font-shaped, shell-flute
of the ugly corner. It was their place.
Like the besom brooms and big hares
hanging in the High Street shops,
it was their place.
I was an American arts fellow,
a veteran of mild exchanges, unimpressive
skirmish.

But it shocked me,
the red remembering wreaths
on the ugly gray, the worn-out
indifferent font of the half-circle,
their public place,
defending the kingdom.
And I forgot
my sole and surviving son wrote
he totaled the car and his left hand,
put up to shield, was sliced and speared
and stabbed to bone, my one son.
In some world's war,
scrolled across gritty documentary screens,
he got shot down, rolled on by tanks,
flat as a cartoon cat—
    (the cartoon cat blinks,
    peels up from the road, inflates, goes on
    to fool the bulldogs, the winking mice).

A son like this, left-handed and articulate,
is missed in a strange place,

and the pimento petals shocked me—
    while
    back home
    the War Mothers sold poppies.

Missing Persons

These venerable picked-over January trees
make a children's jumble of pickup sticks
and blur my long telescoping stare
back to those irritable black bears and swans
and the long jumbling fears
of gingerbread. My twins children rumble
through their yard, torment
the cats, and settle finally to bed
where the same venerable blur of sleep
telescopes their aim, softening
bones, and blood
keeps a steady pickup sticks,
pickup pickup, the hard game going.

I stare down January
unraveling my own picked-over place
and time back where birds ate up the crumbs
and moons smoothed the gravel. I'm little.
It *is* a game.
And I remember rules:

The boy holds out a bone each day,
the blind woman curses, and the girl,
tender in the background,
makes no sudden moves.

Running in Place

Again some deep complaint in the bone,
an old schoolteacher harping, *You could die,
you could, you!* spits like a black pot
laid on my little blond mother's fire.
And when the blood relaxes,
warms up my bones, my hinges,
the dumb dressmaker's doll,
this kettle of renderings I call my legs
hurts. So much for appendages.

I leave much to be desired, as they say,
as my little blond mother said, so I run
miles miles miles miles,
sweat out hot pheromones
and bruise myself like a peach,
reaching deep in her black pot, reaching
the red bubble rendering its worn beat,
thudrun, thudrun,
her old blood thinning
and sick on air, you running woman,
thudrun, thud.

If I run long enough,
hinges swing open, the dressmaker's doll
dissolves and I am a boy,
what my mother wanted, a tough
and indifferent boy
filmed in her own sweat, an inaccurate
rendering warmed up. She would love this,
saying, *I need me a son,*
reaching a towel, dabbing,
I need me somebody,
plunging her last bet on her boy,
who is not her boy, who is me,
running running *outrunning.*

Everything hurts. My body is the worst
and last of the couriers, a dim-witted messenger
keeping her foot to the track
like a match rasped on the grit,
and it all hurts, dissolves, boils down
to the essence, as they say, to the bare facts,
as my little blond mother said,
and I am back to myself, the woman running.

II

Secret Weapons ❧

Good Things

Years go by and good things don't happen.
Like people lost somewhere
between the back door
and the car, gone out into the eider drifts,
just stepped out a minute
in all those breast feathers,
and sinking down, never found,
like those imperfect and quick-frozen people,
I keep goosing my way around.
I'm not lost.
I kept this house for years
looking at you, at crumbs stuck in the cracks,
cobwebs cauling the corners, at our attack
of healthy accomplished children,
the ones with loud obnoxious toys,
green chemistry sets and rockets.

Snowed under all night,
our Christmas trees melted loops
of piquant candy lights, peppermint,
tangerine, turquoise.
I wanted you to come get me,
come plunging through the dark, sowing good things
like seed everywhere, a modern Santa Claus,
taking your martini up and with a twist.

Finally,
I just found the car,
a familiar blind lump in the snow,
the imperfect and irresistible car.

You know I want to hurt
something,
and leave a scar.

Christmas Gothic

Familiar cedars barb the strange sky
thickening on snow
the way custard thickens on egg, and she knows
he's fixing himself up to die
the way he goes on about sleds, wooden ones,
with wet slow runners, *They never get you through the snow,*
they soak it up and stop. They kill you.
She tells him to sit still a minute, listen to her,
be quiet, stick things on the tree.
A little star in his hand,
Hey! he hears something in the yard, *Hey!*
something faster, *Hey!* a sled
flying over his hard white pasture.
Something signifies something,
something multiplies endless worlds
for him to slip through
light and effortless
as custard, and *No wonder! No wonder!*
he points at the phantom sled, *Hey! You see?*

Rough snow mottles his denim
and soaks through to the skin
as she watches him launch some sled,
a remote enchanted figure, a tough old man disquieting
her candled window.
Gathered in their winter pasture,
his uneasy herd stares and darkens the snow.
Then snow whitens him to his knees,
thickens, and swarms down thousands
of bitter bees until he founders a boot at a time,
tangling the cedars with the sled,
and her warm breath splotches
the window as she says like a baby,
keeps saying, dabbling a finger in candleglow,
Dead out yonder, dead.

Hiking the Narrows
for Clyde, 1922-1991

Right outside the powerhouse,
water is subject to sudden rise
and a violent turbulence.
Somebody inside turns a switch
to churn the turbines
to create the suction
to pull you under,
they don't even know you're out there.

This morning,
we stood around watching the old dam
crowd back that impressive water.
The New Year's ground was all spewed up
in icy bouquets, complicated
crystal formations.
I touched a boot to one
and it broke up, literally
seemed to pass out.

What do the hills around here look like?
you asked. I sucked in my breath,
tasting the cold and the tension,
the sudden turbulence. *Like guns*
I thought, *big guns out of rocks,*
secret weapons.
Then I thought things far worse,
for the moment unsafe,
for the moment spewing
out of the powerhouse
and the ground, things pouring
down on us their sudden rise
and violence
from a remote control point.

But before any of this got out,
before I put a boot to the ice,
you said,
They just look like animals,
gazelles and zebras,
all those loping kinds
of things running or grazing,
like Africa on television,
with the fields rising
to the big rocks, like animals.

Delight

Meat eaters,
you believed in meat eaters: Venus fly-traps,
sundews, and pitchers—the rich way they spread their legs,
opened their lips spangled in peril
and licked the struggling bugs—
the way they strangled
everything. You believed, feeling
short hair rise on your neck and love rush
your skin, it was a gift.
But when you tried to lift them from the fragile Carolina bogs,
they resisted like women,
closing their little bitter traps,
leaving sick little drops
on your hand, tight shut, blackening
the dry garden.

What did it take, you raged,
to make these things live with you,
lie down and love you
tenderly tenderly
tongue to tongue
so sweet and so murderous?

The other women from the garden,
common blossoms greedy for sun and air,
spangled the dry hillsides,
and like escaped crazed things,
ate up a world.

Effective Lures

Catfish rise to the top in March
when the water is high and troubled,
stirred up like spring,
and the best baits are alive,
bluegills and redears.
Hook them so they stay alive for hours,
even overnight.
I know a man can shoot flight birds
with a .22. They come tearing
out like bullets, involuntary, a soft flap
to the ground, then die. The gray-eyed
man out of Bierce, out of Owl Creek,
a man of occurrences.

If you take him fishing,
sit well to the middle on rocky points
near deep water where the wind is strong
around sunken timber. Work spinner baits
or a lump of liver, jig and frog combinations,
a long-billed Rebel, yo-yos, whatever.
You will be troubled, the fish
bursting like bullets. So.
Let the gray-eyed man move first.
Remember his .22. Remember his birds.
Remember the deep deep water.

Road Kill

Running on Highway 740,
you tangled up in thorny hard-poxed oranges,
frightening the tar
with tight obnoxious stars.
They bit your ankle, your tough pith
of knuckle and vein too warm
and plain for this comedy—
a fall-in-the-face death. Such oranges
might make you hit Highway 740 hard,
get run over in a pithy mess, *genus*
Philadelphus, the common little brothers
of love, their gentle name.

And such gentleness tightens
to bring you, a modern person, evergreen
and out of breath, Lycra-thighed,
to the one true thing—dying—
what we run for.
It makes me think about Romans
always killing on the move,
and that thing you see in the movies—
the men lock shields on every side and overhead,
making a hard turtle-plate, *advance advance*,
then on the half-step, *kill kill*.
That's something into which all your soft
and dying parts,
head, four legs, and tail
might be pulled, Caesar's *tartaruca*
to repel barbed arrows,
spears, or any two-edged blade
that brings the blood both ways.

A modern person, you just want
to run without stumbling, fumbling
into the murdering wheels.

Roman movies remind you
what waits beside the road and kills
like an old pocked orange dragon
growling
before his wild combustion
swallows you, true death,
mock orange tree,
philadelphia.

Dressing the Loom

I think about you in your Pawley's hammock
strung between two pines, loblollies,
wretched things, but tall enough to lull
the last backyard of your life. Back then
I stared out from the enameled kitchen,
deliberately invading, a cold
surprise attack, you could not know
how well I shot down your
unprotected sleep, the hammock
like a saggy chrysalis, you could not
know how to a hair I destroyed.

This is gospel and forgivable.
And not too long ago,
Penelope brought back a husband
she strung and looped to keep herself together,
tightening the loom, *There!*
then counted up babies, jam, the wedding silver,
her classical practical domesticities, *They should keep*
until he comes, until!

I braided rope, tied off
the confluence of pure unending wool,
stapling the oily fibers, the coats of many colors,
knocking the heddle against my hip,
but this day and everyday,
ten years and ten years,
I remember my silent staring down
who is that man? who?
Before you died, I'd already killed you from the kitchen
while the smell of supper warmed
and sang and you were sleeping.

Cloudless Sulfur, Swallowtail, Great Spangled Fritillary

Out of willows and milkweed and woods around water,
tight tangled places, came her husband's body count.
His atrocities spotted as dice, perfect specimens,
black pansy faces, purple and cream, plain sulfur,
checkerboards, some females
with powdery fringes and starred wings,
they lay under glass in her husband's room,
where she never went if she could help,
except to pull down windows in a rain.
Brutalities pleased him,
these antennae feeble as her own eyelash,
his willful treasures, his dried perfection.
She breathed on the butterflies,
and her breath flexed, then shriveled,
pungent as blue Windex
she sprayed on his mirror. Later,
she slept in the den, forgetting him,
fortunes and blood spattering the TV screen.
Spring Azures tormented her dreams, the tangled array
of Swallowtails, zebra and tiger, black white,
white yellow, blue black blue, pieces
of purple Mourning Cloaks.
Barbarous screams.
His screams.

She woke, face pressed like a waffle, blinking,
her breath no breath, caught in a net, the stinging
unrelenting ether filling up all the space
beyond the moon, between the stars, the upper
upper regions, volatile, colorless, and highly
flammable. A terrible struggle for air.

Target

They slip a black silk blindfold over my eyes.
Rifles snap into place and ten men aim
at the little x
in the middle of me.
It takes ten, or six, or one,
the smallest military
tactical unit detailed to disperse the bullet.
These people are going to shoot me to death.

The whole world's been gunning for me all night,
so I wonder, sweat feeling its way down my leg,
around around around my neck, I wonder
when I'll turn over to wake up,
the tame friendly sag of the bedsprings
displace these assassins,
the coffee machine blink on, my shower pound
reassuringly the mildewed grout
to deliver me out of this.

Somebody walks up, hands me a king-size cigarette
and a match, one last smoke,
then they tie your hands. I know how it goes.
I inhale, eat the smoke's bitter breath.

These people are going to shoot me to death.

Forecast

Suddenly and by surprise
the little gun goes off in my mind
and you are down for the count, villain,
smiling villain, you are bleeding.
Pure pristine immaculate,
a trough of low pressure develops
along the eastern slopes of the Rockies
with cold air spilling south to the plains behind:
these are my careful predictions, the warm
cruel afflictions of all lovers, like weather.
Our storms soak the entire state
of Arkansas.

While long thin threads of pain sprawl through you
and your blood scrawls the floor, I watch,
amazed I know who did this. I did. I shot
the bullets right into your poor old body,
you not even looking. Striking suddenly and by surprise,
I am a terrorist, a quick assassin,
I devour and ruin utterly. My storm system
draws the moist Gulf north
over a glistening cold front
stalled near Arkansas. Listen.
My most significant air pollutant: particulates.
My forecast: no immediate change.

Goat Man & Girl

Late in the afternoon, the goat man, dark-muscled
and strong, a blue tattoo from the Navy,
turns a girl into something. She idles along,
her teenage air sliding through moist meadows,
steady-moving, covering woods and wet places
in flat woody verbena, then he touches her   pure ocarina.
He lays on halfway-violent hands,
pulls her up tight tighter, then sets her free,
kissing that cool air, forcing the green reeds to melody.

He is a god and she is a girl and she likes to let him do things,
her feet in the Cape Fear, her bikini frail as flowers,
then makes up her mind to jump in and scare him.
That will show *him* who kisses somebody,
that will show *him* who pulls up a person.
But her feet jab in the sand off shore
and with bending knees and grabbing fingers,
she feels her frail residual skin turn thin as a reed
played all over by a halfway-violent hand.
She can't move. Just what he wants.
Everything tilts, sways. She tries to break loose.
No use, he cries. *Straighten up*
and remember starboard right and port left
and you'll get back to shore. You won't drown.
I guess he learned that in the Navy, she blinks, I guess
he thinks I'm impressed.

The sun flowers the Cape Fear,
beating a blue tattoo
as his long slow breath powers her jump
away from him right back. *Come here, girl!*
like cool water creeping her legs, dark and strong
as the imperial goat man, the commanding muscle,
You won't drown, the tattoo wounds
her skin indelible colors, camouflage.

And she gulps air, pulls in the steady wind,
feels mouth and fingers fit perfect
to repeat him again again
in weedy permanent verbena, in pure alluring ocarina,
Good music, babe,
and when it's done,
the seeds get eaten by birds
widespread all summer long
blackrush reed cattail.

Inventory

Their scent cool and sweet as dirt,
cold even, almost shocking
and for the moment closed off,
these buds from the hot house
breathe through my refrigerator,
celebrating. Tight, red, wrapped
labia, they wait to take
the measure of me. My arms
reach as long as their stems,
my thin hair spread in feathers
toward one blond side,
waiting and barbed.

Five days later,
open and loose as a cat,
the warm roses ooze petals
toward my breakfast plate
and their measure is a fragrant
smiling invitational threat:
This is how to die. Spread wide open,
celebrate!

III

A Little Scar ❧

The Care and Feeding of Infants

In the habit of a hot summer afternoon,
the old farm, and a visit,
the wind blooms a rich yellow curtain
by your window, your curtain,
your grandmother's window,
a film shadow first light then dark,
lush oil waved on water, the deepest Easter dye.
A little scar on her mirror like an eye,
an asterisk, a star, disturbs you.
The silvered backing is deteriorating,
little hedgehog,
little death. It spreads like a bomb.

Mirrors and windows invite an eye for an eye,
swap and pay back, wrongside out
and upside down. We are they.
Like film shadows dark
where they should be light
and true light nowhere at all, it is plain
they do appall, you mean as in fear, not pain,
you mean as in a cold sweat
when it finally sweeps through you
your grandmother got old and died,
no matter the gingerbread, the hens, the patient
little feedings in the night, her arms pale
around you, the warmest bed: in her own house,
your grandmother is dead,
which means so are you
in her bed of arms, the little feedings,
the hens, and the gingerbread gone stale.

Around outside the house,
cornfields and hens
like second natures
bloom toward the same hot sun

while supersonic jets scar and star
the homely sky,
and your two children,
incomprehensible, play.
When these,
her great-grandchildren,
are hungry, your standing order
is to get up and feed for her
both brother and sister
dark lush elemental gingerbread
rich with eggs she stole from the hens,
your old habit is
patiently
patiently
eat the love of the dead.

The Eagle

Marked man,
he backpacked and trailed,
swam miles through sharks,
killed big crushing snakes and little biting ones
to stand here and get the eagle
put on him in front of these
looking looking people.
These people never
keep their hands off the man,
want him to die for his country,
Jesus All-American, carrying
the ball straight down the ninety-
nine yard line, *looking looking*,
their sucking eyes like sponges,
their big hands hooking the hem
of his garment.

What he really is, your son,
this lone tough star, demands
other sacrifice. Striking
out for territory that way
at Linville Gorge
he rappelled backward
one hundred feet in sheer air.
The double rope wound through
slant-eyed belaying pins
controlled his slide *down down*
the sheer rock, a long fall
to the ground. Nobody
calls this man back,
his cleats gnash the rock
and he's gone.

You're too much
an itinerant multitude, and you

don't dare drop over the side.
But he, the man,
dropped his own hard legs, his rope,
and chanced straight down
the cruel blue and insatiable air
by himself alone, holding
place—
such solitude,
such flair.

Hot Air Balloon

We drove in a big ugly VW van.
We paid our money. We went into the Land
of Oz and like the movie dissolved
Kansas black and white to technicolor
riding hot air balloons and bumper cars
through Dorothy's sideways house.
We tornadoed this amusing Oz.

You stood flexible and merciful,
every hair in those days
raised in a ruffle, not at all fragile,
a little girl readied for red-hot pokers,
for hairline fractures, ground zero,
for razor blades in the apple.
You, like me, could handle anything.
I was the mother. And the bright inscrutable
joying boy was the brother, the brother you baptized,
all things being equal, in your brief
powerful
dream.

Why does this injure me?
The world perjured itself: we went to Oz,
our unnatural natural place. Everything balanced.
The bubble moved to the clear center
of the spirit level, perfectly horizontal,
without deception. We paid our money.
The brother laughed and you did,
and the mother, me. *I'll never forget this!*
I'll never forget this! you marveled
over the tacky Blue Ridge yellow brick road,
Beech Mountain and Hounds Ears,
all an amusement, a theme park, our hot air
continental drift balloon.

Let me point out something.
Strong winds aloft do not allow warm weather
to linger. We stayed together too long, child,
and the chance of rain is scant over Kansas.
A fast-moving disturbance out of the northwest,
especially in higher elevations,
is expected driving hail and tidal surges,
a rapid band of ugly storms,
I'll never forget this,
I'll never forget this! But—

get out of the balloon,
go home.

Birthday

Her angry uncompromising bones
got her up. They mocked the rain coming,
the long cold spell, some high pressure
moving toward the front,
too late to call it off, too late
to take it back. She was what they said,
fifty years of used-up bone and joint,
homesick for the dead, homesick for *herself!*
they jeered, the *girl!*

She shaved her hard perfumed legs,
fastened earrings. Then as she opened
the door, her stubborn brain
took over like a twisting dark tornado
insisting plain enough,
This is you, legs and earrings!
A Frankenstein movie cable-jumping her skull,
Go on, it curled, *you're not old,*
be exotic and irrevocable,
the stunning baby girl!

She went downstairs and for a minute
wanted candles, pink cake, her little blond mother
frowning with lipstick, a dark nylon seam
down the back of each leg,
holding a match, warning, *Keep still!*
for the photographer, his bulbs igniting her face.
She wanted that for a minute. Then.

The clock in the stove struck.
Its little green digital hands totted off
the luminous minutes. And she came back to herself
to hear the tame linoleum kitchen with its crumbs,
its familiar dirts and old perfumes,
say everything was just the same, everything.
She cleaned it up again

and put things back in rooms,
slamming doors, dot dot dotting crumbs
with a wet finger,
her earrings nuzzling like fish
at the surface.

Young Woman in the Shoe

Hours of babies gaudy as pandas
tumble, swell to rhinos, cuddle up
and explode in a rage of little bats
scrambling the rented floor, the green
formica table: her worst dream,
each baby face mews at her,
each fist hooks a bit of skirt
between thumb and wet finger
as she stirs their quick Quaker grits.
She ought to feed them, she ought to.

Before she spreads the table,
the babies spill it, track up her floor
with white desperate paws.
One thing too much hanging on her,
and him, *him!*
her irresistible *him!*
barreling down the sunny interstate,
phoning from the easy truck stops,
Hey, Babe! Whatcha doin, Suge?
So she hits, first them,
then herself, brings the blood,
divides the grits, and ministers
to their enraging and pitiful hunger.
She ought to.

Now bigger bats stud her roof,
pungent as black cloves,
and giant pandas stuff the corner,
while in the bathtub, baby-pink rhinos submerge
to their eyeballs, waiting, *everything dead!*
she did it she did it! her worst dream,
and down the interstate the irresistible
and sunny man returns.

Screech Owl

Her skylights bristle frost
as the house underneath shifts
toward temperatures brought up by the sun.
She knows this Monday, its church bells,
traffics, the bland indifferent
and common little cautions.
She knows what it means, the man beside her,
until an owl, imperative and in between
shivering shivering with great blurred
amber eyes, a hard scarred beak,
shrieks toward her in a dull frayed bed.
She dreads herself.

The dread all tough women have
shivering in themselves, a feathered ball.
She won't know how to tell it.
Maybe the man will say?
The man squints,
cigarette pegged in his teeth,
hints at something long gone.

She *knows*
how her toes might harden
to claws, her flapping arms feather
to reach him. Shivering with speech, she blinks,
almost shrieks against sunlight, and pecks
its bright tatters fraying the contour sheet.

The Dying Off of Your Menfolks, Uncles and Fathers, Brothers, Husbands, and Sons

for James Ross

With the hot green swagger
of summer over, all our hot digging
through dirt and dropping down seeds,
now comes our easing off. The dipper clangs
against our teeth and a wild scuppernong tang
in the water relieves. It's dark,
we can sit on the porch and talk
about men.

They went to Belgium with the Army
where a woman with her cat in Leige
said, *Il ron-ron!*—vibrating
her own verb, *Americans! he purrs,
he likes you!* They stroked that cat
and he slept a shameless trust
in the foreign but familiar sun they shared,
grinding away his throaty delight,
vibratory and exact.

The life of a cat asleep,
that big Belgian cat
with his long shameless bivouac
in the sun, flexing
under the hands
of our men
his trusting lazy dream
and all the green swagger
of our occupying army,
has purred down to one low
vibratory sound,
*Il ron-ron! We are asleep. Something
likes us, we purr.*

We make these sounds
and echo from inside
when we seem to be pleased.
The cat in his cat dream still trusts us,
and like him, we will die
echoing summer facts,
green and throaty,
with our grinding down, our easing off
the familiar porch in the dark
and the wild deep drink of water.

Brown Turkey Figs, a Temptation

Excitable membranes.
Their thumbs in the figs,
the figs slitting, the little seeds shining—
this is the summer they learn
how sweetly those pliable tissues bruise
when you push too hard. Their grandmother
softens toward death and studies them
across the yard, her seeds. And her figs,
the big leaves rough as a turkey foot,
claw their heads. She shrugs forward,
hand to hipbone thin as breath,
like crab shells. Delicate and selectively
permeable, she can allow
one substance, such as blood,
to pass through more easily than another,
such as sugar, such as salt,
and so she shrugs forward
to study the fragile and reckless children,
their hot thumbs plunged in her brown turkey figs.
She will stop them, explain the true fruit
is inside and the thing that falls,
the soft pulpy drop to the hand,
—its curious taste crawls
the tongue, sweet, then so sharp—
oh, is false.

Good Colds

Letting loose fragrances of camphor,
eucalyptus, menthol, the burning oil of clove,
my grandmother jabbed Vicks
down her throat and never gagged.
I longed for the shape she made
against her linen shade, a big
blue-shadowed warmth, nest-builder,
while birds in the chimney
flexed their dark wings, taunting
Does this mean anything?
I thought I might drown,
sitting big-eyed on her bed
like the asthmaed Buddha,
the flanneled congested Jesus.
In the end she layered my lungs
with the same slime, unselfish
and useful, weathered me for whatever
and where, anointed and spiced me
for who and for what breathing,
it does not matter. The dark wings
in the chimney clothed my mind,
the soot fell like snow, and we both
breathed off to bed.
If you hear of such a healer,
if any such healer hears me,
I need to know.

Camera Obscura, the Last Morning

More people die, husband love,
between night and day, in the little obscure time
when dark slips up to the light and stretches,
just catches a breath,
then goes on home
in a camera getting its focus,
fingering the lens, *sharper, sharpest*,
straight home, a shiver all over
like diamonds, like twinkling
all over, and it's done.

I'll die right here in this bed,
you worked yourself to death,
breathed yourself to little pieces,
turning over, bruising
your blood like the red
tissue paper we wrapped
the surprises in for Christmas,
the children's wild, blood-red
surprises, my flash
discharging stars in their faces.

So I'm not surprised to find you gone
and the morning tightening in a camera,
focusing its sharpest picture,
storm clouds and the rain driving down
hard all day and people bringing kind
covered food. *I'll die
right here in this bed*, you said
and I believe you meant this way:
a hard-driving breath
slips off, contracts your dark pupil
to an accurate bull's-eye
privately, secretly,

the blue aperture widens
one more!
and you're gone.

Thoreau at Night

I love a broad margin to my life,
and all night birds flit soundlessly from the room,
and the bloom of the moment showers him
in a cloud thick as his pines and hickories
growing to the window, taking apart the roof,
the cellar hole, breathing
a path back to the great world.
Exact as a star inside the sickle moon inside a vibrant
nictitating membrane, his eye alerts the dark,
feeling the little changes,
the little calibrations, drinking light and air
until he sees the bottom of this place, eternity.
And in the perfect bloom of this moment,
a man who lets things alone,
he rejoices the far dark owls,
a cup bearer to the pond, and drops sleeping, sleeping,
the moon, the pond, the moon.

Near dawn, a thin chill light,
and he is up, still a little afraid of the dark.
Then—outside! the pond with its white sand
and patient scrub of water, back again,
back again—
everywhere he puts his foot, it is spring,
it is morning.